Simone Biles

PARiS 2024
PARi
USA

Simone Biles

Sara Gilbert

Living in THE SPOTLIGHT

CREATIVE EDUCATION
CREATIVE PAPERBACKS

ASTROS
ASTROS
WORLD SERIES

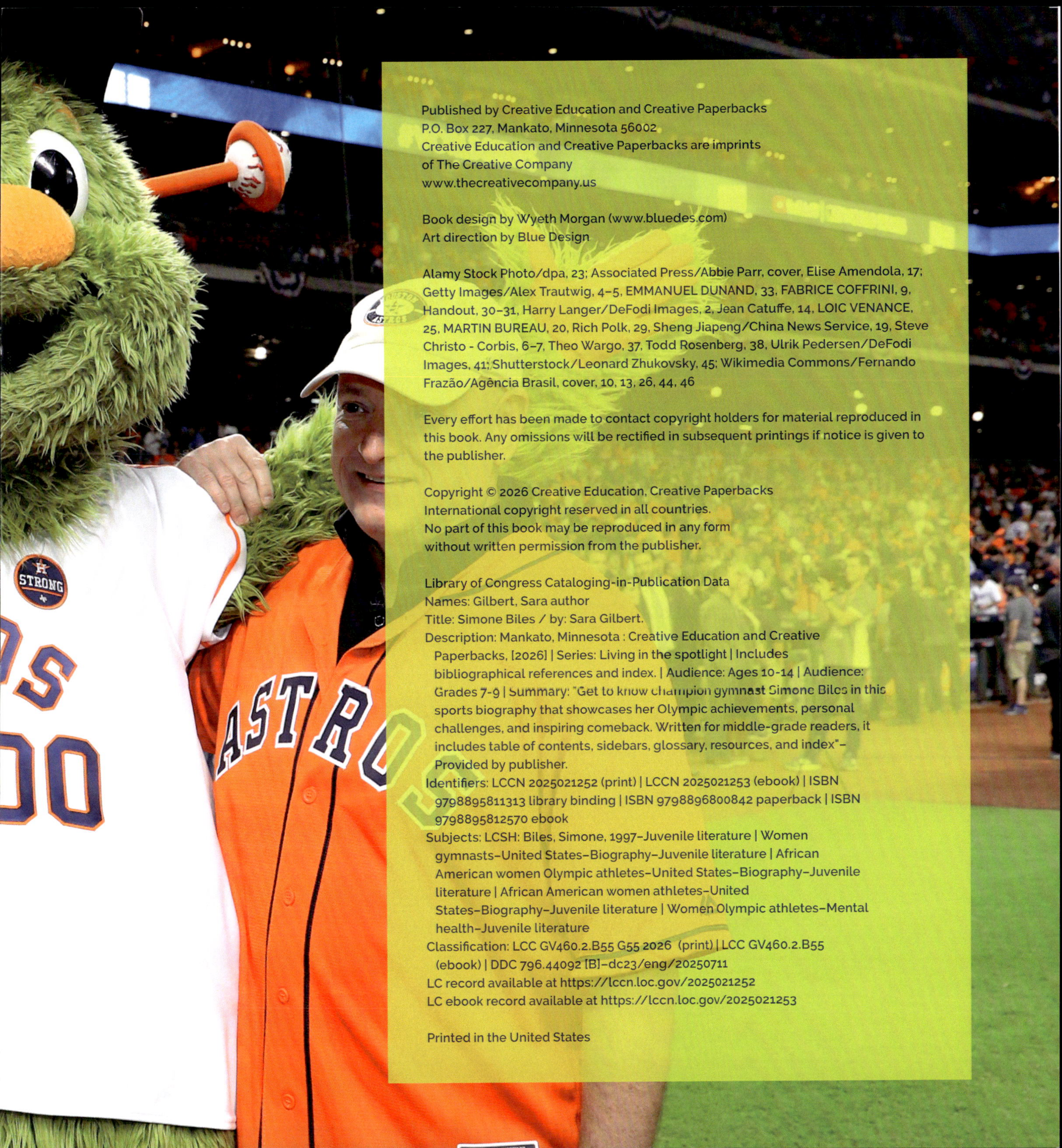

Published by Creative Education and Creative Paperbacks
P.O. Box 227, Mankato, Minnesota 56002
Creative Education and Creative Paperbacks are imprints
of The Creative Company
www.thecreativecompany.us

Book design by Wyeth Morgan (www.bluedes.com)
Art direction by Blue Design

Alamy Stock Photo/dpa, 23; Associated Press/Abbie Parr, cover, Elise Amendola, 17; Getty Images/Alex Trautwig, 4–5, EMMANUEL DUNAND, 33, FABRICE COFFRINI, 9, Handout, 30–31, Harry Langer/DeFodi Images, 2, Jean Catuffe, 14, LOIC VENANCE, 25, MARTIN BUREAU, 20, Rich Polk, 29, Sheng Jiapeng/China News Service, 19, Steve Christo - Corbis, 6–7, Theo Wargo, 37, Todd Rosenberg, 38, Ulrik Pedersen/DeFodi Images, 41; Shutterstock/Leonard Zhukovsky, 45; Wikimedia Commons/Fernando Frazão/Agência Brasil, cover, 10, 13, 26, 44, 46

Library of Congress Cataloging-in-Publication Data
Names: Gilbert, Sara author
Title: Simone Biles / by: Sara Gilbert.
Description: Mankato, Minnesota : Creative Education and Creative Paperbacks, [2026] | Series: Living in the spotlight | Includes bibliographical references and index. | Audience: Ages 10-14 | Audience: Grades 7-9 | Summary: "Get to know champion gymnast Simone Biles in this sports biography that showcases her Olympic achievements, personal challenges, and inspiring comeback. Written for middle-grade readers, it includes table of contents, sidebars, glossary, resources, and index"– Provided by publisher.
Identifiers: LCCN 2025021252 (print) | LCCN 2025021253 (ebook) | ISBN 9798895811313 library binding | ISBN 9798896800842 paperback | ISBN 9798895812570 ebook
Subjects: LCSH: Biles, Simone, 1997–Juvenile literature | Women gymnasts–United States–Biography–Juvenile literature | African American women Olympic athletes–United States–Biography–Juvenile literature | African American women athletes–United States–Biography–Juvenile literature | Women Olympic athletes–Mental health–Juvenile literature
Classification: LCC GV460.2.B55 G55 2026 (print) | LCC GV460.2.B55 (ebook) | DDC 796.44092 [B]–dc23/eng/20250711
LC record available at https://lccn.loc.gov/2025021252
LC ebook record available at https://lccn.loc.gov/2025021253

Printed in the United States

USA

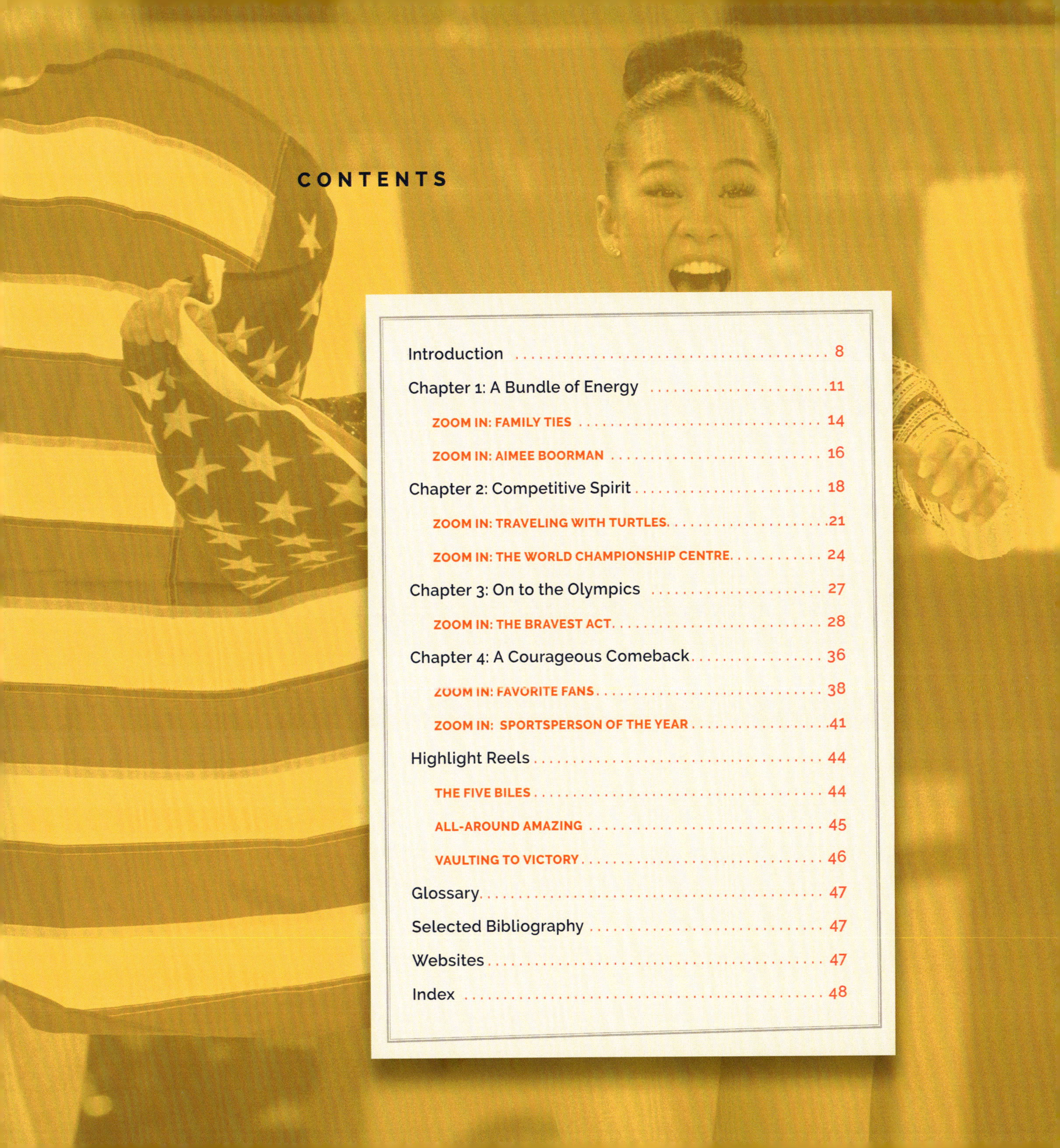

CONTENTS

Introduction

Simone Biles is posed at the edge of the floor. She flexes her feet and takes a deep breath as her name is announced over the loudspeaker. The crystal studs in her blue Team USA **leotard** twinkle in the lights of the arena. As bright as they are, they can't compare with the smile on her face when she raises her arms over her head to signal the start of her floor exercise routine. Although her concentration is evident, that brilliant smile reminds everyone watching the 2024 Olympic Games both in the arena and on TV that Biles is having fun.

As the music starts, she begins her routine, bending and twisting as she finds the starting point for her first tumbling pass. She pushes off, the muscles in her legs propelling her across the floor. She drops into a roundoff, flips backwards and then powers upward to do a series of twists in the air before landing solidly, both feet planted on the floor. The crowd cheers as she sticks the landing and throws her arms in the air.

But Biles isn't done yet. She continues moving through her routine. She seems perfectly at ease as she flips and twists while flying through the air. She kicks, spins, and flexes. All the while, she smiles.

She finishes as the music ends, her legs stretched out on the floor. Then she bounces back up, beaming, as she waves happily to the crowd. Everyone is cheering for her. She's performed an almost flawless routine, worthy of a gold medal!

Biles makes a difficult and beautiful sport look easy.

CHAPTER 1:

A Bundle of Energy

Simone Biles was first introduced to gymnastics because it was raining. Her summer daycare center in Houston, Texas, had planned a field trip to a country farm, but the rain made that impossible. So instead, they took the children down the street to Bannon's Gymnastix.

Six-year-old Biles, who had already been bouncing, flipping, and tumbling on the trampoline at her parents' home, was delighted by what she saw when she walked in. Gymnasts were doing handsprings on the vault. They were flipping on the balance beam and swinging around the bars.

Biles wanted to do what they were doing. Although she was small for her age, she had a huge amount of energy. She was also a strong little girl who already had muscular legs. She started tumbling, jumping, and trying to imitate the other girls. Then her older brother Adam, who was working at the daycare that summer, encouraged her to do a backflip. She did—but she did a little twist and added a second flip before landing on her feet.

That move caught the attention of Veronica "Ronnie" Bannon, who was watching Biles from across the room. She could tell that the tiny little girl with a huge smile had a lot of energy, as well as a natural **aptitude** for gymnastics. She sent a letter home for Biles's parents, encouraging them to sign her up for a class. And starting the next week, both Biles and her little sister Adria were registered for two 45-minute sessions a week.

Biles's sister didn't love gymnastics and soon dropped out to join Girl Scouts. But Biles flourished. Her raw ability caught the eye of Aimee Boorman, who was one of the gym's coaches. Boorman moved Biles to the United States of America Gymnastics (USAG) Junior Olympic program, where she would be able to progress through 10 skill levels and compete against other gymnasts locally, regionally, and eventually, nationally.

Biles loved competing and moved through the levels with relative ease. The first hiccup came when she moved to **regulation**-height bars, which are higher than what she first trained on. Because she was so small, with a short stature and little hands, the uneven bars were a challenge for her. One day she was practicing a move called a giant, which is swinging 360 degrees around the high bar. After two rotations, she lost her grip and toppled over. Instead of landing on the soft foam piled beneath the bars, she bounced off and rolled to the side, landing on the concrete. She wasn't seriously hurt, but her confidence was

Biles in her Team USA leotard at the 2016 Rio Olympics.

USA

ZOOM IN: FAMILY TIES

Biles and her sister Adria were adopted by their grandparents, Ron and Nellie Biles, in November 2003. Ron and Nellie had started taking care of the girls, as well as their older sister Ashley and brother Tevin, in 2000. Their mom, Shanon, was struggling to take care of them and they all ended up in foster care. Ron and Nellie brought the four of them from their hometown of Columbus, Ohio, to Texas. Ashley and Tevin were eventually adopted by Ron's sister Harriet, who lived in Cleveland, Ohio, Biles has called Nellie and Ron mom and dad since the adoption became final.

shaken. She didn't want to get back on the bars, but her coaches told her to keep working on them.

Biles kept practicing the move until she felt comfortable doing it. But even then, she struggled taking her level seven test—and not just on the bars. She also made mistakes on the beam and couldn't stick her landings on her tumbling routine. She failed on her first try. But the disappointment of failing made her practice more seriously for the next try. She knew she needed to focus. Her hard work paid off and she passed on her second attempt.

As she moved up, she spent more and more time at the gym working on her skills. By the time she was 11 years old and working through level nine, she was spending up to four hours a day training. She was consistently winning medals at gymnastic meets and had begun to think seriously about the future. Specifically, she was thinking about the 2012 Olympics, which would take place in London. Biles wanted to compete as part of Team USA. But she knew it was impossible—and not because she wasn't talented enough. Olympic athletes had to be at least 16 in the year of the competition, and Biles would turn 15 on March 14, 2012. She would have to wait another four years to be eligible.

In 2008, she was frustrated that her first Olympic opportunity was still eight years away. So much could change in that much time. She wrote about it in the five-subject notebook that she used as a journal. "I don't know if I will make it," she wrote. But then she added one more sentence: "I want to go the farthest I can."

Biles knew that she had to push herself to become an **elite** gymnast. She needed to perform well at national meets. If she did, she might be noticed by Márta Károlyi, who was the national USAG team coordinator. She and her husband, Béla Károlyi, ran a gymnastics training center in Huntsville, Texas. An invitation to the Károlyis' **developmental** camp could launch a career. Biles and Coach Boorman decided to increase her hours at the gym. She started going for two hours before school every day, then again after school as well. She was at the gym for 30 hours a week.

All of that work helped her do well at the Houston National **Invitational** in 2010. She placed first on both the floor and the vault and was third overall. But when Coach Boorman sent video from the competition to Márta Károlyi, Károlyi wasn't interested yet. She said that Biles needed to improve on the bars.

Biles worked on her bar routine for the rest of the season. Her coach pushed her to improve her skills and become more

ZOOM IN: AIMEE BOORMAN

Aimee Boorman started doing gymnastics when she was six years old. She started coaching at 13 to earn extra money. But by the time she started college, she knew she wouldn't continue with the sport. When she started missing it, she decided to try coaching again. In 1996, she took a job at Bannon Gymnastix in Houston, Texas. That's where she met Biles. In 2005, she became Biles's coach. Boorman coached Biles for more than 10 years, including during the 2016 Olympics, when she was the head coach of the U.S. women's gymnastics team. She later also served as the head coach of the Netherlands' women's gymnastic team.

Biles defies gravity with her impressive routines.

consistent, but she also encouraged her to have fun. That formula seemed to work. At the end of the season, Biles qualified for the Junior Olympics Nationals event in Dallas, Texas. She won first on floor and third all-around at Nationals and was the U.S. Challenge Pre-Elite All-Round Champion for 2010. Both Biles and her coach were sure that Márta Károlyi would soon reconsider her decision.

CHAPTER 2:

Competitive Spirit

Biles and her Team USA teammates celebrate their Olympic win.

Biles was 14 years old when she arrived in Riverside, California, to compete in the Gliders National Elite Qualifier competition in February 2011. She was just four feet, eight inches (1.2 m, 20.3 cm) tall, but she was strong. And she was determined. She knew that winning at Gliders would give her an opportunity to compete at the American Classic meet at the Károlyi Ranch later that year. If she did well there, she had a chance to go to Nationals and to make the 2011 women's junior team—her ultimate goal.

At the Gliders event, Biles nailed her second vault and her floor routine. She wobbled on the beam and didn't feel like her bars were perfect either. But when the final scores were posted, she had taken first place on the vault and, surprisingly, first place all-around. That meant she was headed to the American Classic. It also meant that her coach had new video to send to Márta Károlyi. This time,

USA

ANTWERP 2013
WORLD CHAMPIONSHIPS
USA

ZOOM IN: TRAVELING WITH TURTLES

When Biles traveled for gymnastics competitions, she packed a few of her favorite turtle figurines along with her leotards and other gear. And everywhere she went, she looked for a new turtle to bring home with her as well. She had begun collecting turtle figurines as a young gymnast, when her mom started calling her "Little Turtle." It was meant as a loving reminder to go at her own pace and not worry about keeping up with others. Eventually, her mom started giving Biles a tiny turtle before every meet, and she kept special "lucky" turtles tucked in her bag.

A young Biles poses with her winning medal at the 2013 AT&T American Cup.

Biles received an invitation to a five-day developmental camp at the Károlyi ranch.

The camp was a challenge for Biles. The **conditioning** work and skills training were exhausting. She had to work harder than ever before. But she made new friends and improved her vault and beam performance so much that she placed first in each of those events in the American Classic. Her final score was good for third place overall—and high enough to qualify for the upcoming Visa National Championship.

Biles worked hard to prepare for Nationals. She challenged herself to learn a new skill for bars called the Tkatchev. She was excited to go to St. Paul, Minnesota, for the meet. But when the final scores were announced, she tried hard to hide her disappointment. Biles had finished 14th. That meant she didn't qualify to be one of the 13 members of the national women's junior team.

It was hard to rebound from that crushing blow. Biles decided to be homeschooled so that she could spend more hours at the gym, but she struggled to get her attitude back on track. She argued with her coaches and with her dad, who was teaching her at home. But she stayed focused on her goal and worked hard to improve her skills—especially a vault called the Amanar, which she did so well that she earned first on vault in every competition during the 2012 season. Biles qualified for Nationals again, and this time, she was prepared. She earned third all-around at Nationals, which cemented her place on the junior national team.

Her first competition as part of that team was the American Cup in 2013. She and Katelyn Ohashi were selected to represent the United States in the event. It was the first time Biles was performing in a televised meet. She was so nervous that her stomach hurt. Although she did well in almost every event, she crashed to the floor during her beam routine and ended up finishing second, behind Ohashi. But she kept working. Biles traveled internationally with the team and helped them take gold in competitions in Italy and Germany—and she placed first in vault, beam, and floor as well.

In 2013, Biles turned 16. That meant she was no longer a junior. She was now competing as a senior alongside the stars of the 2012 Olympics—Gabby Douglas, Aly Raisman, and Kyla Ross. But when she performed poorly at her first senior meet in 2013, she had a heart to heart with Márta Károlyi, who told her that she needed to respect her talent more. Biles also met with a sports psychologist for the first time. Sports psychologists help athletes address the mental aspects of competition. He reminded Biles that she should have fun with gymnastics.

That advice worked. Biles took first place at the 2013 P&G National Championship and was then selected to be part of the

Biles embraces Kyla Ross.

32

U.S. World Championship team. She would compete in Antwerp, Belgium as part of Team USA at the highest level shy of the Olympics.

No one expected Biles to win in her first Worlds competition. But she had perfected a new floor exercise that included a double layout, with her body straight and her legs together as she flipped twice in the air, followed by a half twist before landing. She performed that move at Worlds, and it became known as the Biles, because she was the first to do it. And in part because of that, Biles ended the competition with the highest total score. She became the first Black gymnast to win the all-around gold in the World Championship.

As she was training for the 2014 competition season, her long-time coach decided to leave Bannon Gymnastix. Coach Boorman asked Biles and her sister Adria, who had returned to gymnastics, to follow her to a new gym. That new gym was the World Champions Centre (WCC), a 52,000-square-foot (4,831 square meter) facility that Ron and Nellie Biles built in Spring, Texas.

It took two years to complete the WCC, so in the meantime Biles worked with Coach Boorman in a rented gym and at the Károlyi Ranch in Huntsville. By now, she was focused on getting to the 2016 Olympics, and she worked hard to make sure she would earn a spot on the team. She repeated as the all-around winner at both the U.S. and World Championships in 2014 and

ZOOM IN: THE WORLD CHAMPIONSHIP CENTRE

When Boorman left Bannon Gymnastix, the Biles family did, too. But instead of finding a new gym, they built their own. They found a four-acre plot not far from the family's home in Spring, Texas, and spent two years building an enormous gym. Although it was designed as a place where Biles and other elite gymnasts could train, it was also big enough to offer classes in tumbling, taekwondo, cheerleading, kickboxing, and more. It had rows of windows on every side, which flooded the building with natural light. It opened to the public in 2015 and now employs almost 70 people.

Biles focuses ahead of her 2021 Tokyo Olympics routine.

became the first female gymnast to win a third consecutive all-around gold at the World Championships in 2015.

As Biles started training for the 2016 Olympic Trials in the newly opened WCC in 2015, she had an important decision to make. She could either choose to go to college or to become a **professional** gymnast. She was being recruited by several universities, including the University of California, Los Angeles (UCLA), but she was also receiving offers from **sponsors** who would pay her lots of money if she turned professional. In July 2015, she decided to go pro.

USA

CHAPTER 3:

On to the Olympics

Before the Olympic Trials in 2016, Raisman gave Biles some advice. Raisman had won two gold medals in the 2012 Olympics, and, at 22, seemed much older and wiser than 19-year-old Biles. She told her teammate to go to bed early, to remember to breathe, and to look at the Olympics as just another World Championship event.

Those words of wisdom helped Biles place first all-around at the Olympic Trials in San Jose, California, which ensured her position on Team USA alongside Douglas, Raisman, Madison Kocian, and Laurie Hernandez. All that was left between her and the 2016 Olympics in Rio de Janeiro, Brazil, was a 10-day training camp at the Károlyi Ranch. At the end of the camp, the families of the gymnasts were invited to come down for an open house and to wish them well. Biles's mom sat with her and asked her to make a promise.

Biles performing her floor routine at the 2016 Rio Olympics.

ZOOM IN: THE BRAVEST ACT

The Olympics weren't the only reason gymnasts were in the news in 2016. That summer, a newspaper in Indiana published the first story about Larry Nassar, a longtime member of the medical staff for USA Gymnastics. Nassar was accused of inappropriately touching young athletes at the Károlyi Ranch. Eventually, more than 200 gymnasts bravely came forward to report the abuse that had occurred, including Biles. In 2021, Biles courageously testified before Congress about her experience. "I don't want another young gymnast, or Olympic athlete, or any individual to experience the horror that I and hundreds of others have endured," she said.

"Promise that you'll do your best," she said. "This is your dream, Simone, so go out there and live it with everything you've got. And don't forget to have fun."

Not long after that, when Biles walked out with the team to begin the qualification round of the 2016 Olympics in Brazil, she heard a familiar voice yelling, "Go, Simone!" It was her mom, sitting with the rest of the family in the stands. Seeing them calmed her nerves and helped her earn first place in the qualifying round and one of two Team USA spots in the all-around competition. Raisman secured the other.

Two days later, Biles and her Olympic teammates competed in the team competition in Rio de Janeiro. Each one of them was almost flawless in their routines. Together, they won a gold medal for Team USA. Although they were excited to stand on the podium and have medals placed around their necks, the event finals

Biles was an honoree at the Marie Claire Young Women's Honors in 2016, a movement dedicated to women's empowerment.

Biles, fellow Olympians Michael Phelps and Aly Raisman, and actress Olivia Munn performed on an All-Star episode of *Lip Sync Battle.*

and the all-around competition were yet to come. There was still more work to be done.

On the day of the all-around competition, Biles woke up feeling good. She carefully outlined her eyes with gold glitter and applied a subdued lipstick. She put on her favorite leotard, which had sheer sleeves dotted with sparkling crystals, red-and-white stripes on the sides and a shiny blue bodice covered in white stars. She and Raisman walked together to the bus that took them to the gymnastics arena and gave each other encouraging messages. But it wasn't until she heard her mom's voice yelling, "You've got this, Simone!" that she felt the knots in her stomach settle down.

Biles's first rotation was the vault, where she did the Amanar move that had been her hallmark. She scored an impressive 15.866 and was in first place. She had a great bar routine with a solid **dismount,** but scored only 14.966 and fell to second. Then came the beam, where Biles had planned for a difficult double twisting, double tuck dismount. She nailed it and the crowd erupted. Her score of 15.433 gave her the lead once again. Going into the final rotation on the floor, she only needed a score of 13.833 to win gold. She didn't have to be perfect—but she wanted to be. She received a score of 15.933, which assured her of the all-around gold medal.

But the Olympics wasn't over yet. Biles still had the opportunity to compete in the individual event finals. She wobbled on the beam and had to grab it with both hands, which led to an automatic one-point deduction. But she still won the bronze medal

Biles with her Olympic gold medal, showing that hard work pays off.

UNITED STATES
OLYMPIC TEAM

for beam based on the difficulty of her routine and the rest of her execution. She also became the first American woman to win a gold medal on the vault. She won another gold for her floor exercise. At the end of the Olympic Games, the other athletes on Team USA voted for Biles to carry the American flag into the closing ceremony.

When she returned home, Biles decided to take a break from training and competing. She announced that she wouldn't compete for 18 months to give her body a break and allow herself time to have fun. But she seemed to pick up where she left off when she returned to competition in 2018, sweeping all four individual events at the U.S. Gymnastics Championships and winning her fifth national all-around title. In 2019, she won her fifth all-around gold at the World Championships and set a new record with a total of 25 World Championship medals.

The 2020 Summer Olympic Games in Tokyo were delayed because of the COVID-19 pandemic, which started in the spring of 2020. In June 2021, Biles was again named to the women's gymnastics team—this time with a whole new group of gymnasts: Jordan Chiles, Sunisa "Suni" Lee, Grace McCollum, Jade Carey, and McKayla Skinner.

But something wasn't right in Tokyo. Biles had several missteps during her events in the qualifying round. She qualified to compete in the all-around and in the finals in all four individual events, but she wasn't on top of her game. After the qualifiers, she posted on social media that she was feeling "the weight of the world" on her shoulders.

The trouble became apparent during the team finals, when Biles struggled with her usually flawless Amanar move on the vault. Instead of completing two-and-a-half twists, she only managed one and a half and almost fell on the landing. She left the competition floor after that, and shortly after withdrew for the team competition. She said that she had "the twisties," a mental condition in which gymnasts feel disoriented during **aerial** moves. She said she needed to prioritize her mental health.

Biles eventually withdrew from every other event except for individual balance beam, which took place on the last day of gymnastics competition. Although she modified her routine to avoid twists, she still placed high enough to earn a bronze medal. That, combined with the silver team medal that she received in Tokyo, put her total medal count at seven—tied with Shannon Miller for the most medals won by an American gymnast.

The aftermath of Biles' decision to withdraw from competition in the 2021 Olympics was brutal. Although many fans, media outlets, and other gymnasts defended her decision, many others were highly critical. She was called a quitter and a national embarrassment. One radio host insisted that she apologize to her fellow gymnasts. Another described her as selfish, immature, a shame to the country, and a sociopath. It was no surprise, then, that Biles needed a break from gymnastics when she returned home.

CHAPTER 4:

A Courageous Comeback

By the fall of 2022, Biles was ready to think about gymnastics again. When she returned to Texas after the Olympics, she had taken a complete break from the sport to focus on her mental health. She started doing **therapy** to talk through her challenges. During her two-year **hiatus**, Biles announced her engagement to Jonathan Owens, a professional football player who she had met on a dating app in 2020.

In 2022, she was also honored with the Presidential Medal of Freedom, the youngest person ever to receive the honor. President Joe Biden gave it to her in honor of her athletic achievements, as

Biles and her husband Jonathan Owens at the 2025 Met Gala.

ZOOM IN: FAVORITE FANS

Biles married Owens in a small civil ceremony on April 6, 2023, and then celebrated with a destination wedding in Mexico a month later. Since then, the couple has wholeheartedly supported each other's athletic endeavors. Biles was often seen wearing green and gold at Lambeau Field while Owens was playing for the Green Bay Packers. After he was signed by the Chicago Bears, she started attending games at Soldier Field. And Owens has attended her meets as well, including the 2024 Olympics. He dressed in red, white, and blue and cheered loudly with the rest of the Biles family from the stands.

well as her advocacy for athlete mental health, for children in foster care, and for victims of sexual assault.

When she finally felt ready to return to the gym, her primary goal was simply to get back into shape. By January 2023, she was practicing twice a day at the World Championship Center, working with new coaches Laurent and Cécile Landi. And as Biles turned 26 in March of that year, she started thinking about returning to competition. She decided that after her wedding to Owens in May, she would officially make her comeback.

Her first competition was the U.S. Classic in August of 2023. Despite not competing for two years and two days, she appeared to pick up where she had left off. She won the all-around title by a full five points and took first in both floor and beam. That performance qualified her for the U.S. Championships, where she also won the all-around title as well as floor and beam titles. Biles became the first gymnast—male or female—to win eight all-around gold medals in the U.S. Championships.

Next up was the World Championships—her first international competition since the Olympics. Worlds were held in Antwerp, Belgium, in 2023, just as they had been when she first qualified in 2013. And just like she had back then, Biles won the all-around gold—her sixth such medal—as well as gold in floor and beam, and silver in vault. At 26, she had been the oldest woman to win the all-around gold in the U.S. Championships, and the oldest competitor at Worlds in 50 years. "I think I'm in better shape than I was in 2021," she told reporters after the meet. "Mentally and physically."

Biles had been worried that fans wouldn't welcome her back after what happened in Tokyo. But when she started competing again, she saw young girls holding up hand-lettered signs saying "You've got this, Simone Biles" and "Go Simone!" She heard entire arenas cheering for her. That outpouring of support encouraged her to consider working toward the 2024 Olympics in Paris. And with all-around wins at both the U.S. Classic and the U.S. Championships in 2024, it looked likely that she would be competing in Paris.

The Olympic Trials were held in June at the Target Center in Minneapolis, Minnesota. Many of the competitors were familiar to Biles, including several of her teammates from the Tokyo Games. She won the all-around title and placed first in floor, second on bars, and fourth on beam, and she earned a spot representing the United States on Team USA in the 2024 Olympics. She became only the fourth female gymnast ever to compete at three Olympic games, and the first to do so since 2000.

ZOOM IN: SPORTSPERSON OF THE YEAR

Every year, *Sports Illustrated* labels one athlete the "sportsperson of the year." For 2024, the magazine bestowed that title on Biles. She had earned it by virtue of winning gold again (three times) at the 2024 Olympics—but also for her impact on gymnastics and on sports in general. The magazine lauded her ability to make a comeback after her withdrawal from competition in Tokyo and the light she shone on the importance of mental health. But most importantly, the article noted, they were honoring her because she was able to question whether she could do it again—and then take off at a run and do it.

Biles arrived in Paris in late July with familiar teammates: Carey, Chiles, and Lee, all of whom had competed in Tokyo, and Hezly Rivera, who was making her first Olympics appearance. In the qualification round, the team finished in first place, and Biles qualified for the all-around (as did Lee) and for all four individual events.

The competition gave Biles an opportunity to practice the work she had done to support her mental health during her break from gymnastics. She told reporters that she was meeting with her therapist when needed—including before the team and all-around finals. "The Olympics is such a draining process for the athletes when it's multiple days of competition, so you definitely have to be on top of your mental, as well as your physical health," she said.

"A couple years ago, I didn't think I'd be back here at an Olympic Games, so competing and then walking away with four medals...I'm pretty proud of myself."

Team USA took first in the team final, and Biles topped teammate Lee and Brazilian Rebeca Andrade to win gold in the all-around. Biles had made a mistake during her bar routine, but made up for it with flawless performances on beam and floor to finish the competition with the highest total score. She became only the third gymnast to ever win two Olympic all-around titles, and the first to do it in non-consecutive competitions.

It was no surprise when Biles took gold in the vault, after performing one of five unique moves that have been named after her (the Biles II, which combines a Yurchenko with a double pike). But what was surprising was what happened on the balance beam: Biles fell off the beam and then incurred additional deductions for not appropriately saluting the judges at the end of the routine. It was the first time that she had not medaled in the beam during either the Olympics or Worlds. During her floor exercise, she uncharacteristically stepped out of bounds twice, which resulted in a six-tenths deduction. Although she still won the silver medal, it was the first time she hadn't earned gold on floor as well.

"Obviously, it wasn't my best performance, but at the end of the day, whoever medaled, medaled," she said after the Games. "A couple years ago, I didn't think I'd be back here at an Olympic Games, so competing and then walking away with four medals...I'm pretty proud of myself."

From her first introduction to gymnastics as a six-year-old to her Olympic performance at the age of 27, Biles has proven how much she loves the sport—and how much she loves to have fun. Only she knows whether she will compete again on the Olympic stage. Even if she doesn't, her energetic performances and tremendous skills will be remembered forever.

Highlight Reel

THE FIVE BILES

In gymnastics, moves are named after the first person to complete them flawlessly in an approved competition. Biles has five moves that bear her name—two for the vault (Biles and Biles II), two for the floor (Biles and Biles II), and one for the balance beam (Biles).

Her first named move was the backward double layout with a half-twist that she added to her floor exercise in the 2013 World Championships. In 2019, she introduced a triple-double—two flips and three tucked twists—at the World Championships. The Biles II, as it's now known, has a higher difficulty rating than the first.

She debuted her first vault move at the 2018 World Championships. It's a roundoff from the springboard that leads directly to a half-turn onto the vault, followed by two twists before landing. The second was named after she performed it during the 2023 World Championships, although she had been working on it since 2021. Like the first, it starts with a roundoff from the springboard; it then goes into a back handspring onto the vault and finishes with two straight-leg back flips.

Biles's beam move is a complicated dismount. It consists of a double twisting backflip before sticking the landing. That move was named after she performed it at the 2019 World Championships.

Only two gymnasts have more moves named after them: Svetlana Khorkina, who has eight, and Nellie Kim, who has seven. Both are from Russia.

ALL-AROUND AMAZING

Gymnastic competitions often include multiple events for gymnasts to participate in. They may compete as a team and on individual apparatuses: vault, bars, floor and beam. They may also compete for the all-around title, which is given to the gymnast with the highest overall score in all four events.

Biles has a total of 17 all-around medals: nine in the U.S. Championships, six in the World Championships and two in the Olympics.

One of her most exciting all-around victories came during the 2016 Olympics. She had started with an excellent vault—pushing solidly off the table, spinning twice with her body fully extended and adding a half twist before landing. Although she took a step, her score was high enough to put her in first place.

Then came the uneven bars, which has always been the hardest apparatus for Biles. But she felt like every skill flowed seamlessly and that she flew higher than ever before. She even stuck the dismount. But because the difficulty level wasn't very high, her score dropped her to second place.

The third rotation was beam. Biles was in the zone and completed each of the skills perfectly. Even her landing was flawless. Her score was high enough to push her back to first place.

The last event was floor—which is where Biles feels most confident. She knew as she was completing her tumbling passes, flipping, twisting, and sticking her landings, that she had nailed it. Her score of 15.933 was the highest of the competition! It was also all she needed to win the all-around gold in Rio.

VAULTING TO VICTORY

Biles is known for her excellence on vault. She has consistently medaled for her vault performances in competitions, including at the 2016 Olympics, where she won the gold. So when she struggled to complete her vault and then fell during the 2021 Olympics, it was clear that something was wrong.

Biles had "the twisties," and it took two years away from gymnastics and working with therapists for her to be ready to try that kind of movement again.

So when Biles approached the apparatus again during the 2024 Olympics in Paris, it was understandable that she was concerned about what might happen this time. She turned to Chiles, her teammate and friend who was standing next to her, and whispered, "What if it happens again?"

But instead of freezing up, Biles was mentally ready. She signalled to the judges and then started to run the 82 feet (25 m) to the vault table. She cartwheeled onto the vault table, pushed her body into the air, then performed two complete flips with her legs perpendicular to her body in the pike position. It was almost perfect, aside from the small step she took on the landing.

Her performance earned thunderous applause from the audience. It also earned her a gold medal, her second Olympic gold for vault. But she wasn't ready to say it was her last. "Never say never," she said to reporters after the event.

Glossary

aerial—a maneuver that involves moving through the air

apparatus—a piece of equipment used for a specific act or exercise

aptitude—a natural ability for something

conditioning—the process of training to be prepared for competition

developmental—related to the growth and development of someone's abilities

dismount—a move in which a gymnast jumps off of a piece of equipment to end a routine

elite—belonging to a select group that is superior in skills and abilities to others

foster care—a temporary living arrangement for children whose families are unable to safely take care of them

hiatus—a brief pause or break in an activity

invitational—an event open only to invited participants

leotard—a close fitting, one-piece outfit designed to be worn while exercising or performing gymnastics

professional—a person engaged in a sporting or artistic activity for payment

regulation—official

sponsor—a person or corporation who pays to support someone or something

therapy—the treatment of mental health conditions through talking and other methods

Selected Bibliography

Apstein, Stephanie, "Simone Biles is SI's 2024 Sportsperson of the Year," *Sports Illustrated.* Jan. 2, 2025.

Biles, Simone, *Courage to Soar: A Body in Motion, a Life in Balance,* Zondervan, Grand Rapids, Michigan: 2016.

Biography: Simone Biles. https://www.biography.com/athletes/simone-biles. Jan. 5, 2025

Blackwell, Geoff and Ruth Hobday. *I Know This to Be True: Simone Biles,* Chronicle Books, San Francisco, California, 2020.

Boorman, Aimee. *The Balance: My Years Coaching Simone Biles,* Abrams Press, New York: 2025.

Macur, Juliet, "To Become the Goat, Simone Biles First Had to Be a Turtle," *New York Times.* Aug. 5, 2024.

Websites

Olympics
https://olympics.com/en/athletes/simone-biles
Learn more about Simone Biles's three Olympic appearances.

Simon Biles
https://simonebiles.com
Visit Simone Biles' own webpage to learn more about her as a person.

USA Gymnastics
https://members.usagym.org/pages/athletes/nationalTeamWomen.html?id=164887
Learn more about Simone Biles's records and achievements in gymnastics.

Index